The Art of

Espresso Martinis

A Journey of Indulgence Recipes

E Coffee Finder

EcoffeeFinder.com

"The Art of Espresso Martinis: A Journey of Indulgence Recipes" is the ultimate companion for those who appreciate the finer things in life—the perfect blend of coffee and spirits, the joy of crafting exquisite cocktails, and the shared moments of connection and celebration.

Join Sarah and David on their extraordinary adventure and unlock the secrets of the Espresso Martini, one sip at a time.

Contents

Meet Sarah and David

Intro

In the world of fine dining and social gatherings, there is an art to creating the perfect ambiance, where flavors dance on the palate and conversations flow effortlessly. Among the myriad culinary delights, the Espresso Martini stands as an elegant blend of sophistication and indulgence, captivating the hearts and taste buds of couples who share a passion for both entertainment and coffee. Join us on a delightful journey as we unveil the artistry and allure of Espresso Martinis and the captivating story of a couple who found joy in mastering this craft.

A Shared Passion

Meet Sarah and David, a couple deeply in love with each other and with the art of entertaining. Their shared interest in hosting lavish gatherings became the foundation of their relationship. Sarah, a talented mixologist with an innate ability to create delightful concoctions, and David, an avid coffee enthusiast with an appreciation for the intricacies of flavors, embarked on a journey to explore the realms of cocktail craftsmanship.

The Quest for Perfection

Driven by a desire to offer their guests an exceptional experience, Sarah and David turned their attention to the Espresso Martini—a cocktail renowned for its harmonious blend of rich espresso and velvety vodka. They dedicated countless hours to researching the origins, experimenting with different coffee beans, and refining the cocktail's balance of flavors.

Their quest led them to discover the magical alchemy that occurs when coffee and spirits intertwine. The vibrant bitterness of the coffee merged seamlessly with the smooth sweetness of the vodka, creating an extraordinary union that delighted the senses. With each sip, they transported their guests to a realm where coffee and cocktails converged, leaving them with a lingering, enchanting taste.

The Artistic Presentation

As Sarah and David continued to refine their Espresso Martini recipe, they realized that presentation was as crucial as the flavor itself. They delved into the art of garnishing, experimenting with chocolate shavings, coffee beans, and even a sprinkle of gold dust. Their creations became a feast for the eyes, inviting guests to immerse themselves fully in the magical ambiance they meticulously curated.

Sharing the Love

Sarah and David's passion for Espresso Martinis began to transcend their own enjoyment. They decided to share their expertise with others who yearned to master this captivating art form. They organized intimate cocktail workshops, where couples and friends could gather to learn the secrets of the perfect Espresso Martini.

These workshops became a platform for forging new friendships, exchanging stories, and inspiring creativity. The couple reveled in the joy of witnessing others' eyes light up as they took their first sip of a meticulously crafted Espresso Martini. It was a testament to the power of blending entertainment and coffee into a mesmerizing experience.

The art of entertainment and coffee beautifully intertwines in the world of Espresso Martinis. Through the dedication and passion of couples like Sarah and David, this iconic cocktail has become more than a drink—it's a symbol of the love and craftsmanship that goes into creating unforgettable moments. So, the next time you savor an Espresso Martini, remember the story of this enchanting couple, who turned their shared passion into an art form, and let the magic of their journey transport you to a world of flavor and delight.

A Summer Soirée: Where Espresso Martinis Steal the Show

Step into the world of Sarah and David, a couple whose love for entertainment, coffee, and the art of Espresso Martinis knows no bounds. As summer casts its warm embrace, they embark on a delightful journey of creating the ultimate dinner parties that showcase the enchanting allure of Espresso Martinis. Join us as we dive into their vibrant lifestyle, meet their eclectic group of friends, and witness the meticulous preparations for a night of culinary and mixological wonders.

The Invitation

With the arrival of summer, Sarah and David extend their invitations to their closest friends, eager to share their passion for Espresso Martinis. The invitations, carefully crafted with a touch of elegance, carry an air of anticipation for the upcoming soirée. As the guests receive their personalized cards, excitement and curiosity begin to brew.

The Perfect Venue

Sarah and David meticulously choose a stunning outdoor venue for their summer dinner parties. A charming garden, adorned with fairy lights and vibrant flowers, sets the stage for an enchanting evening. They carefully arrange cozy seating areas where conversations can flow freely, and a dedicated cocktail bar becomes the focal point, ready to deliver the magic of Espresso Martinis.

The Gourmet Feast

For Sarah and David, the culinary experience is as

important as the cocktails. They collaborate with a renowned chef to curate a gourmet feast that complements the rich and complex flavors of Espresso Martinis. The menu showcases a symphony of flavors, from delicate canapés to delectable entrées, each dish meticulously paired to enhance the cocktail experience.

Part 4: The Friends Arrive

As the sun begins to set, the friends arrive one by one, adorned in their finest summer attire. Sarah and David's social circle is a tapestry of personalities—a mix of artists, food enthusiasts, and fellow cocktail aficionados. There's Emily, a talented painter whose vibrant artwork adds a splash of color to their gatherings, and Alex, a renowned food critic who appreciates the intricate marriage of taste and presentation.

The Cocktail Ritual

With the stage set and their friends gathered Sarah and David gracefully step behind the cocktail bar, ready to showcase their mastery of the Espresso Martini. They explain the origins and intricacies of the cocktail, captivating their audience with their passion and knowledge. Each drink is meticulously prepared, ensuring every guest receives a perfectly balanced blend of espresso, vodka, and sweetness.

The Magic Unveiled

As the first sip of the Espresso Martini touches their guests' lips, a symphony of delight ensues. The rich, velvety notes of the cocktail intertwine with the laughter and animated conversations, creating a harmonious ambiance. Sarah and David's meticulous preparations and unwavering dedication have transformed their summer soirée into an unforgettable sensory experience.

Creating Memories

Throughout the evening, the guests revel in the magic of Sarah and David's hospitality. They share stories, engage in lighthearted banter, and forge connections that extend beyond the boundaries of the soirée. Each moment becomes a snapshot in time, a cherished memory created by the seamless blend of entertainment, culinary delights, and the captivating art of Espresso Martinis.

Sarah and David's summer dinner parties are a testament to their unwavering passion for the art of entertainment, coffee, and the allure of Espresso Martinis. With each meticulously crafted event, they weave a tapestry of flavors and friendships, leaving a lasting impression on all who attend. So, the next time you find yourself raising a glass to the captivating union of coffee and cocktails, remember the vibrant lifestyle of this extraordinary couple, who transformed the ordinary into the extraordinary and turned simple gatherings into unforgettable experiences.

As the summer nights wane, Sarah and David's legacy lives on. Their friends, inspired by their love for entertainment and the art of Espresso Martinis, begin to host their own soirées, carrying forward the passion and creativity that were ignited in those magical evenings. The art of blending coffee, mixology, and companionship becomes a shared tradition among their circle, a celebration of life's simple pleasures.

And so, the story continues, as new friendships are formed, flavors are explored, and the beauty of Espresso Martinis becomes a cherished part of the collective memory. Sarah and David's legacy lives on through the laughter, clinking glasses, and the captivating aroma that fills the air, reminding everyone of the magic that can be created when passion and creativity intertwine.

So, whether you find yourself hosting an intimate gathering or attending a grand celebration, remember the tale of Sarah and David, the couple who painted a vibrant tapestry of flavors and friendship through their love for entertaining and the art of Espresso Martinis. Raise your glass high, savor each sip, and let the spirit of their story inspire you to create your own moments of enchantment, where coffee, cocktails, and the beauty of human connection come together in perfect harmony.

Cheers to the art of entertainment, coffee, and the captivating world of Espresso Martinis—where flavors awaken the senses, and love and friendship are forever celebrated.

Welcome to a World of Indulgence

Welcome to a world of indulgence, where the velvety elixir of espresso dances gracefully with the spirit of vodka, and the air is filled with an intoxicating aroma that tantalizes the senses. Step into a realm where every sip is an invitation to embrace the artistry and sophistication of Espresso Martinis.

Welcome to a world where the clinking of glasses mingles with laughter, and the symphony of flavors takes center stage. It is a place where the boundaries between coffee and cocktails blur, and a new form of liquid poetry emerge.

In this realm of indulgence, a single cocktail becomes a gateway to an enchanting experience—a sensory journey that ignites the taste buds and awakens the spirit. Here, the rich, robust notes of espresso merge harmoniously with the smooth, subtle sweetness of the finest vodka, crafting a libation that transcends mere refreshment.

Welcome to a world where artisans of flavor like Sarah and David have devoted their lives to perfecting the craft of Espresso Martinis. With a delicate balance of precision and creativity, they have unlocked the secrets of blending the finest coffee beans with the purest spirits, infusing each cocktail with a touch of their passion and artistry.

In this world, every detail matters—the selection of the beans, the careful extraction of the espresso, the precise measurements of vodka and liqueurs, and the artful garnishes that adorn each glass. It is a realm where the presentation is as mesmerizing as the flavors themselves, where a beautifully crafted cocktail is a testament to the love and dedication that went into its creation.

So, prepare to embark on a journey of indulgence, where every sip brings you closer to a realm of refined pleasures. Join us as we explore the captivating world of Espresso Martinis, where the alchemy of coffee and spirits takes form, and where moments of bliss are forged in each elegantly crafted glass.

Welcome to a world of decadence, sophistication, and the intoxicating allure of Espresso Martinis. Get ready to lose yourself in a symphony of flavors, as we unravel the secrets and stories behind this exquisite libation. Let the journey begin.

Exploring the Art of Mixology

In the realm of Espresso Martinis, Sarah and David are revered as maestros of mixology, crafting liquid masterpieces that evoke awe and delight. They are the embodiment of passion, creativity, and unwavering dedication in the pursuit of the perfect cocktail.

With a twinkle in their eyes and a shared love for entertaining, Sarah and David have embarked on a never-ending quest to elevate the art of mixology. They dive deep into the realm of flavors, exploring the nuances of coffee varietals, experimenting with unique combinations of spirits, and pushing the boundaries of creativity.

Their journey takes them to remote coffee plantations, where they immerse themselves in the world of beans, cherishing each step of the coffee-making process. From the careful selection of ripe coffee cherries to the meticulous roasting and grinding, they understand that the quality of the coffee is the heart and soul of an exceptional Espresso Martini.

Back in their cozy haven, Sarah and David transform their kitchen into a laboratory of flavors. They meticulously measure and mix, adjusting the ratios with scientific precision. Their hands move gracefully as they shake, stir, and strain, infusing each cocktail with a touch of their artistic flair.

But their artistry extends beyond the ingredients. They understand that presentation is paramount—a feast for the eyes is as important as the tantalizing flavors. Sarah and David craft their own signature glassware, hand-painted with delicate patterns that echo the beauty and sophistication of their cocktails. Every detail is meticulously considered to create an immersive experience, where aesthetics merge seamlessly with taste.

Their journey is not without challenges. Countless hours are spent experimenting, fine-tuning, and even experiencing occasional failures. But Sarah and David persevere, drawing inspiration from the alchemy of flavors and the joy of sharing their creations with friends and loved ones.

It is this spirit of sharing that truly sets them apart. Their home becomes a haven for those seeking an escape from the ordinary, a place where the curious gather to witness the art of mixology unfold. The laughter and animated conversations that fill the air are a testament to the warm and inviting atmosphere that Sarah and David effortlessly create.

As word of their extraordinary Espresso Martinis spreads, they are invited to host guest appearances at renowned cocktail bars and culinary events. They graciously accept these opportunities to share their passion with a wider audience, spreading their love for the art of mixology far and wide.

In their world, Espresso Martinis are not just cocktails; they are an expression of love, creativity, and the joy of bringing people together. Sarah and David's journey is a testament to the power of pursuing one's passion, transforming it into an art form, and sharing it with the world.

So, step into their world, where each sip of an Espresso Martini is a glimpse into the artistry and dedication that Sarah and David pour into their craft. Join them on this extraordinary adventure as they continue to push the boundaries of mixology, one captivating cocktail at a time. Cheers to the artists of flavor, the creators of memories, and the enchanting world of Espresso Martinis.

Unveiling the Magic of Espresso Martinis

Prepare to embark on a journey of flavor, as Sarah and David unveil their most treasured creations—a collection of 20 extraordinary Espresso Martini recipes that showcase the depth and versatility of this captivating libation. Each cocktail is a testament to their unwavering dedication, meticulous craftsmanship, and boundless creativity.

Within these pages, you will discover a symphony of flavors that takes you from the traditional to the avant-garde, from classic combinations to unexpected pairings that will leave you delightfully surprised. Sarah and David have poured their hearts and souls into curating a selection that will intrigue, inspire, and captivate even the most discerning palates.

From the first sip, you will be transported to a world where coffee and spirits converge in perfect harmony. Each recipe tells a unique story, an exquisite blend of ingredients that balances the rich bitterness of espresso with the smooth sweetness of spirits. The cocktails are crafted with precision and care, ensuring that every element harmonizes flawlessly.

But this collection is more than just a compilation of recipes. Sarah and David invite you into their creative process, sharing insights into their inspiration, the flavor profiles they explored, and the stories behind each cocktail. They delve into the art of garnishing, providing tips and techniques to elevate your presentation and make each drink a work of art.

As you flip through the pages, you will find classics reimagined, unexpected flavor combinations that challenge conventions, and nods to cultures and traditions from around the world. Sarah and David's expertise and passion shine through as they invite you to join them on this sensory adventure.

Whether you are a seasoned mixologist, an aspiring home bartender, or simply someone with an appreciation for exceptional cocktails, this collection promises to ignite your imagination and expand your repertoire. With these recipes, you will have the tools to create moments of indulgence, impress and delight your guests, and elevate your own love affair with Espresso Martinis.

So, stay tuned as we delve into the enchanting world of Espresso Martinis and unlock the secrets behind Sarah and David's captivating creations. Each recipe will be unveiled, revealing the careful balance of flavors, the innovative twists, and the sheer artistry that make their cocktails truly extraordinary.

Join us as we embark on this remarkable journey of flavor, where the magic of Espresso Martinis unfolds, one inspired recipe at a time. Get ready to experience a collection that will awaken your senses, ignite your creativity, and leave an everlasting impression. Let the adventure begin.

Recipes Part 1: Classic Delights

Classic Espresso Martini:

1. Indulge in the timeless elegance of the Classic Espresso Martini. This iconic cocktail combines the rich flavors of vodka, coffee liqueur, and freshly brewed espresso, creating a harmonious blend that's both smooth and invigorating.

Ingredients:
- 2 oz vodka
- 1 oz coffee liqueur
- 1 oz espresso
- 1/2 oz simple syrup

Instructions:

1. Fill a cocktail shaker with ice cubes.
2. Add vodka, coffee liqueur, espresso, and simple syrup.
3. Shake vigorously for about 15 seconds.
4. Strain the mixture into a chilled martini glass.
5. Garnish with coffee beans, if desired.

Vanilla Espresso Martini:

1. Experience a touch of luxury with the Vanilla Espresso Martini. The velvety vanilla vodka adds a luscious and fragrant note to the robust espresso and coffee liqueur, resulting in a sophisticated and irresistible cocktail.

Ingredients:

- 2 oz vanilla vodka
- 1 oz coffee liqueur
- 1 oz espresso
- 1/2 oz simple syrup

Instructions:

1. Fill a cocktail shaker with ice cubes.
2. Add vanilla vodka, coffee liqueur, espresso, and simple syrup.
3. Shake well for approximately 20 seconds.
4. Strain the mixture into a martini glass.
5. Optionally, garnish with a vanilla bean or a sprinkle of ground vanilla.

Chocolate Espresso Martini:

1. Satisfy your chocolate cravings with the decadent Chocolate Espresso Martini. The combination of chocolate vodka, coffee liqueur, and espresso creates a heavenly drink that's a true delight for chocolate lovers.

Ingredients:

- 2 oz chocolate vodka
- 1 oz coffee liqueur
- 1 oz espresso
- 1/2 oz simple syrup

Instructions:

1. Fill a cocktail shaker with ice cubes.
2. Pour chocolate vodka, coffee liqueur, espresso, and simple syrup into the shaker.
3. Shake vigorously for about 15-20 seconds.
4. Strain the mixture into a chilled martini glass.
5. Optionally, dust the drink with cocoa powder for an extra touch of chocolate.

Recipes Part 2: Creative Twists

Hazelnut Espresso Martini:

1. Embrace the nutty and aromatic flavors of the Hazelnut Espresso Martini. The indulgent blend of hazelnut liqueur, coffee liqueur, and espresso offers a delightful twist to the classic recipe, delivering a velvety smooth, and irresistible concoction.

Ingredients:

- 2 oz hazelnut liqueur
- 1 oz coffee liqueur
- 1 oz espresso
- 1/2 oz simple syrup

Instructions:

1. Fill a cocktail shaker with ice cubes.
2. Add hazelnut liqueur, coffee liqueur, espresso, and simple syrup.
3. Shake well for approximately 20 seconds.
4. Strain the mixture into a martini glass.
5. Optionally, garnish with a toasted hazelnut on the rim of the glass.

Salted Caramel Espresso Martini:

1. Discover the perfect balance of sweet and salty with the Salted Caramel Espresso Martini. This tantalizing cocktail combines the rich notes of caramel vodka, coffee liqueur, espresso, and a touch of sea salt, creating a captivating and luxurious treat.

Ingredients:

- 2 oz caramel vodka
- 1 oz coffee liqueur
- 1 oz espresso
- 1/2 oz simple syrup
- Pinch of sea salt

Instructions:

1. Fill a cocktail shaker with ice cubes.
2. Pour caramel vodka, coffee liqueur, espresso, simple syrup, and a pinch of sea salt into the shaker.
3. Shake vigorously for about 15-20 seconds.
4. Strain the mixture into a chilled martini glass.
5. Optionally, drizzle caramel sauce on top and sprinkle a pinch of sea salt for garnish.

Coconut Espresso Martini:

1. Escape to a tropical paradise with the refreshing Coconut Espresso Martini. The fusion of coconut rum, coffee liqueur, espresso, and a hint of sweetness transports you to an island getaway, offering a delightful twist to the classic recipe

Ingredients:

- 2 oz coconut rum
- 1 oz coffee liqueur
- 1 oz espresso
- 1/2 oz simple syrup

Instructions:

1. Fill a cocktail shaker with ice cubes.
2. Add coconut rum, coffee liqueur, espresso, and simple syrup to the shaker.
3. Shake vigorously for about 15 seconds.
4. Strain the mixture into a chilled martini glass.
5. Optionally, garnish with a toasted coconut rim or a sprinkle of shredded coconut.

Recipes Part 3: Flavors of the Seasons

Irish Espresso Martini:

1. Experience the luck of the Irish with the delightful Irish Espresso Martini. The smooth and creamy Irish cream liqueur, combined with coffee liqueur, espresso, and a touch of sweetness, creates a heavenly drink that's sure to please.

Ingredients:

- 2 oz Irish cream liqueur
- 1 oz coffee liqueur
- 1 oz espresso
- 1/2 oz simple syrup

Instructions:

1. Fill a cocktail shaker with ice cubes.
2. Pour Irish cream liqueur, coffee liqueur, espresso, and simple syrup into the shaker.
3. Shake well for approximately 20 seconds.
4. Strain the mixture into a martini glass.
5. Optionally, dust the drink with a pinch of cocoa powder or top with whipped cream.

Spiced Espresso Martini:

1. Add a touch of warmth and spice to your cocktail repertoire with the Spiced Espresso Martini. The infusion of spiced rum, coffee liqueur, espresso, and a hint of sweetness provides a comforting and aromatic twist to the classic recipe.

Ingredients:

- 2 oz spiced rum
- 1 oz coffee liqueur
- 1 oz espresso
- 1/2 oz simple syrup

Instructions:

1. Fill a cocktail shaker with ice cubes.
2. Add spiced rum, coffee liqueur, espresso, and simple syrup to the shaker.
3. Shake vigorously for about 15-20 seconds.
4. Strain the mixture into a chilled martini glass.
5. Optionally, garnish with a cinnamon stick or a sprinkle of ground nutmeg.

Mocha Espresso Martini:

1. Unleash the irresistible combination of coffee and chocolate with the luscious Mocha Espresso Martini. The harmonious blend of vodka, coffee liqueur, chocolate liqueur, espresso, and a touch of sweetness delivers a delightful treat for your senses.

Ingredients:

- 2 oz vodka
- 1 oz coffee liqueur
- 1 oz chocolate liqueur
- 1 oz espresso
- 1/2 oz simple syrup

Instructions:

1. Fill a cocktail shaker with ice cubes.
2. Pour vodka, coffee liqueur, chocolate liqueur, espresso, and simple syrup into the shaker.
3. Shake well for approximately 20 seconds.
4. Strain the mixture into a martini glass.
5. Optionally, garnish with a chocolate-covered espresso bean.

Recipes Part 4: Unique Experiences

Mint Chocolate Espresso Martini:

1. Indulge in the refreshing and indulgent Mint Chocolate Espresso Martini. The combination of chocolate vodka, coffee liqueur, espresso, a hint of sweetness, and a splash of peppermint schnapps creates a delightful and invigorating drink reminiscent of a minty chocolate treat.

Ingredients:

- 2 oz chocolate vodka
- 1 oz coffee liqueur
- 1 oz espresso
- 1/2 oz simple syrup
- Splash of peppermint schnapps

Instructions:

1. Fill a cocktail shaker with ice cubes.
2. Add chocolate vodka, coffee liqueur, espresso, simple syrup, and a splash of peppermint schnapps to the shaker.
3. Shake vigorously for about 15 seconds.
4. Strain the mixture into a chilled martini glass.
5. Optionally, garnish with a sprig of fresh mint or a chocolate wafer.

Raspberry Espresso Martini:

1. Experience a burst of fruity goodness with the vibrant Raspberry Espresso Martini. The infusion of raspberry vodka, coffee liqueur, espresso, and a touch of sweetness creates a tantalizing cocktail that's both refreshing and full of flavor.

   Ingredients:

   - 2 oz raspberry vodka
   - 1 oz coffee liqueur
   - 1 oz espresso
   - 1/2 oz simple syrup
   - Fresh raspberries for garnish

   Instructions:

   1. Fill a cocktail shaker with ice cubes.
   2. Pour raspberry vodka, coffee liqueur, espresso, and simple syrup into the shaker.
   3. Shake well for approximately 20 seconds.
   4. Strain the mixture into a martini glass.
   5. Garnish with fresh raspberries on a cocktail pick.

Gingerbread Espresso Martini:

1. Capture the cozy flavors of the holiday season with the delightful Gingerbread Espresso Martini. The combination of vodka, coffee liqueur, espresso, and a dash of gingerbread syrup creates a warm and aromatic drink that will transport you to a winter wonderland.

Ingredients:

- 2 oz vodka
- 1 oz coffee liqueur
- 1 oz espresso
- 1/2 oz gingerbread syrup
- Gingerbread cookie crumbs for rimming

Instructions:

1. Rim the edge of a martini glass with gingerbread cookie crumbs.
2. Fill a cocktail shaker with ice cubes.
3. Add vodka, coffee liqueur, espresso, and gingerbread syrup to the shaker.
4. Shake vigorously for about 15 seconds.
5. Strain the mixture into the prepared martini glass.

Recipes Part 5: Exotic Escapes

Orange Espresso Martini:

1. Elevate your cocktail experience with the zesty and invigorating Orange Espresso Martini. The fusion of vodka, coffee liqueur, espresso, and a touch of orange liqueur offers a refreshing twist to the classic recipe, perfect for citrus enthusiasts.

   Ingredients:
   - 2 oz vodka
   - 1 oz coffee liqueur
   - 1 oz espresso
   - 1/2 oz orange liqueur
   - Orange zest for garnish

   Instructions:

   1. Fill a cocktail shaker with ice cubes.
   2. Pour vodka, coffee liqueur, espresso, and orange liqueur into the shaker.
   3. Shake well for approximately 20 seconds.
   4. Strain the mixture into a martini glass.
   5. Garnish with a twist of orange zest.

Almond Espresso Martini:

1. Indulge in the rich and nutty flavors of the Almond Espresso Martini. The infusion of amaretto liqueur, coffee liqueur, espresso, and a hint of sweetness creates a velvety smooth cocktail with a delightful almond undertone.

   Ingredients:

   - 2 oz amaretto liqueur
   - 1 oz coffee liqueur
   - 1 oz espresso
   - 1/2 oz simple syrup

   Instructions:

1. Fill a cocktail shaker with ice cubes.
2. Add amaretto liqueur, coffee liqueur, espresso, and simple syrup to the shaker.
3. Shake vigorously for about 15-20 seconds.
4. Strain the mixture into a chilled martini glass.
5. Optionally, garnish with a toasted almond on the rim of the glass.

Coconut Vanilla Espresso Martini:

1. Embark on a journey of tropical indulgence with the tantalizing Coconut Vanilla Espresso Martini. The blend of coconut vodka, coffee liqueur, espresso, and a touch of vanilla syrup creates a creamy and exotic cocktail that will transport you to a sun-soaked paradise.

Ingredients:

- 2 oz coconut vodka
- 1 oz coffee liqueur
- 1 oz espresso
- 1/2 oz vanilla syrup

Instructions:

1. Fill a cocktail shaker with ice cubes.
2. Pour coconut vodka, coffee liqueur, espresso, and vanilla syrup into the shaker.
3. Shake well for approximately 20 seconds.
4. Strain the mixture into a martini glass.
5. Optionally, garnish with a vanilla bean or a sprinkle of shredded coconut.

Recipes Part 6: Unexpected Delights

Cinnamon Espresso Martini:

1. Awaken your senses with the aromatic and spicy Cinnamon Espresso Martini. The infusion of cinnamon vodka, coffee liqueur, espresso, and a hint of sweetness creates a captivating cocktail that's perfect for those who crave a little extra warmth. '

Ingredients:

- 2 oz cinnamon vodka
- 1 oz coffee liqueur
- 1 oz espresso
- 1/2 oz simple syrup
- Cinnamon stick for garnish

Instructions:

1. Fill a cocktail shaker with ice cubes.
2. Add cinnamon vodka, coffee liqueur, espresso, and simple syrup to the shaker.
3. Shake vigorously for about 15-20 seconds.
4. Strain the mixture into a chilled martini glass.
5. Garnish with a cinnamon stick for an extra touch of aroma.

Peanut Butter Espresso Martini:

1. Delight your taste buds with the unique and irresistible Peanut Butter Espresso Martini. The fusion of peanut butter vodka, coffee liqueur, espresso, and a touch of sweetness delivers a creamy and indulgent drink that will satisfy any peanut butter lover.

Ingredients:

- 2 oz peanut butter vodka
- 1 oz coffee liqueur
- 1 oz espresso
- 1/2 oz simple syrup

Instructions:

1. Fill a cocktail shaker with ice cubes.
2. Pour peanut butter vodka, coffee liqueur, espresso, and simple syrup into the shaker.
3. Shake well for approximately 20 seconds.
4. Strain the mixture into a martini glass.
5. Optionally, rim the glass with crushed peanuts or garnish with a peanut butter cup.

Coconut Rum Espresso Martini:

1. Escape to a tropical oasis with the luscious Coconut Rum Espresso Martini. The fusion of coconut rum, coffee liqueur, espresso, and a touch of sweetness offers a refreshing and delightful twist to the classic recipe, transporting you to a beachside paradise.

Ingredients:

- 2 oz coconut rum
- 1 oz coffee liqueur
- 1 oz espresso
- 1/2 oz simple syrup

Instructions:

1. Fill a cocktail shaker with ice cubes.
2. Pour coconut rum, coffee liqueur, espresso, and simple syrup into the shaker.
3. Shake well for approximately 20 seconds.
4. Strain the mixture into a martini glass.
5. Optionally, garnish with a toasted coconut rim or a sprinkle of shredded coconut.

Cherry Espresso Martini:

1. Experience a burst of fruity elegance with the tantalizing Cherry Espresso Martini. The infusion of cherry vodka, coffee liqueur, espresso, and a hint of sweetness creates a vibrant and sophisticated cocktail that's perfect for special occasions.

Ingredients:

- 2 oz cherry vodka
- 1 oz coffee liqueur
- 1 oz espresso
- 1/2 oz simple syrup
- Maraschino cherry for garnish

Instructions:

1. Fill a cocktail shaker with ice cubes.
2. Add cherry vodka, coffee liqueur, espresso, and simple syrup to the shaker.
3. Shake vigorously for about 15 seconds.
4. Strain the mixture into a chilled martini glass.
5. Garnish with a maraschino cherry on a cocktail pick.

Recipes Part 7: A Taste of Paradise

Coconut Rum Espresso Martini:

1. Escape to a tropical oasis with the luscious Coconut Rum Espresso Martini. The fusion of coconut rum, coffee liqueur, espresso, and a touch of sweetness offers a refreshing and delightful twist to the classic recipe, transporting you to a beachside paradise.

Ingredients:

- 2 oz coconut rum
- 1 oz coffee liqueur
- 1 oz espresso
- 1/2 oz simple syrup

Instructions:

1. Fill a cocktail shaker with ice cubes.
2. Pour coconut rum, coffee liqueur, espresso, and simple syrup into the shaker.
3. Shake well for approximately 20 seconds.
4. Strain the mixture into a martini glass.
5. Optionally, garnish with a toasted coconut rim or a sprinkle of shredded coconut.

Maple Bacon Espresso Martini:

1. Indulge in a unique and flavorful experience with the unforgettable Maple Bacon Espresso Martini. The infusion of bacon-infused bourbon, coffee liqueur, espresso, and a touch of maple syrup creates a smoky, sweet, and savory cocktail that's a true delight for adventurous palates.

Ingredients:
- 2 oz bacon-infused bourbon
- 1 oz coffee liqueur
- 1 oz espresso
- 1/2 oz maple syrup
- Crispy bacon for garnish

Instructions:

1. Fill a cocktail shaker with ice cubes.
2. Add bacon-infused bourbon, coffee liqueur, espresso, and maple syrup to the shaker.
3. Shake vigorously for about 15 seconds.
4. Strain the mixture into a chilled martini glass.
5. Garnish with a crispy bacon strip for a unique twist.

Conclusion: Reflecting on the Journey

As we come to the end of our journey through the world of Sarah and David, we pause to reflect on the remarkable path they have traversed—a journey fueled by their unwavering love for Espresso Martinis and their shared passion for creating unforgettable experiences.

Throughout their adventure, Sarah and David have not only perfected their craft of mixology but have also woven a tapestry of memories with their friends and family. Countless evenings have been spent in the warm embrace of their home, where laughter, stories, and the clinking of glasses have blended harmoniously.

Their collection of 20 remarkable Espresso Martini recipes has become a testament to their creativity, expertise, and boundless imagination. Each cocktail carries a story—a moment in time when friends gathered, conversations flowed, and the magic of Sarah and David's hospitality brought people closer together.

There was the night when Emily, the talented painter, shared her latest masterpiece—a canvas awash with vibrant colors inspired by the flavors of an Espresso Martini infused with citrus and herbs. The cocktail became a muse, igniting creativity and forging a deeper connection between art and mixology.

Then there was the time when Alex, the food critic, embarked on a culinary exploration, pairing each Espresso Martini with a unique dish, enhancing the interplay of flavors and textures. The collaboration was a testament to the power of friendship and the joy of discovering new horizons.

And let us not forget the cherished family gatherings, where Sarah and David passed down their knowledge and love for Espresso Martinis to the next generation. They watched with pride as their children carefully measured ingredients, shook cocktails with miniature shakers, and tasted the fruits of their labor. It was a moment of continuity, where the legacy of love and flavor was entrusted to the hands of the future.

As we reflect on Sarah and David's journey, we are reminded that life's most treasured moments are not only found in the perfection of a cocktail but in the connections we forge and the memories we create. Through their love of Espresso Martinis, they have opened their hearts and homes, inviting others to share in the beauty of their craft.

Their journey is a testament to the power of passion, creativity, and the bonds formed over a shared love of artful libations. Sarah and David have shown us that when we pursue our passions with dedication and joy, we can create experiences that transcend the ordinary, and transform simple gatherings into extraordinary celebrations.

So, as we bid farewell to Sarah and David's world of Espresso Martinis, we carry with us the lessons they have taught us—the importance of craftsmanship, the joy of hospitality, and the magic of bringing people together through the art of mixology.

May their journey inspire us to unlock our own creative potential, share our passions with others, and savor every sip of life's indulgences. Cheers to Sarah and David, the keepers of the Espresso Martini legacy, and to the beautiful memories they have gifted us along the way.

In the closing of Sarah and David's enchanting tale, we find ourselves captivated by the enduring magic of their love for Espresso Martinis. The journey they embarked upon, filled with flavor and camaraderie, continues to inspire us as we reflect on the profound impact they have had on their friends, family, and even the wider community.

It was during one of their summer dinner parties, where their backyard was transformed into a captivating oasis of lights and laughter, that something truly remarkable unfolded. As the sun dipped below the horizon, casting a golden glow across the faces of their guests, Sarah and David unveiled a surprise—a personalized Espresso Martini recipe for each person in attendance.

The excitement was palpable as their friends eagerly exchanged recipes, discussing the unique flavors and ingredients chosen to reflect their personalities. The joyous conversations that followed were a testament to the way in which Sarah and David's passion for mixology had touched the lives of those around them.

Inspired by the couple's dedication and expertise, their friends began experimenting with their own variations of Espresso Martinis, each one a testament to their personal journeys and the influence of Sarah and David's artistry. These intimate gatherings, now infused with a newfound sense of creativity, became cherished traditions where friends took turns showcasing their latest concoctions, sparking friendly competition and inspiring further exploration.

Beyond their immediate circle, Sarah and David's impact reached even greater heights. They were invited to host masterclasses and workshops, where enthusiasts from far and wide could learn from their expertise. Their shared knowledge and contagious enthusiasm ignited a spark within others, creating a ripple effect that spread the love and appreciation for Espresso Martinis across borders and cultures.

In the midst of their whirlwind journey, Sarah and David remained steadfast in their commitment to inclusivity. They ensured that their gatherings were open and welcoming, embracing diversity and celebrating the unique perspectives that each person brought to the table. Their home became a safe haven, where people from all walks of life could come together, united by their love for Espresso Martinis and the warmth of genuine human connection.

And so, as we bid adieu to Sarah and David, we carry their spirit of inclusivity and passion for the craft in our own hearts. We are inspired to create our own gatherings, to share our love for cocktails, and to celebrate the beauty of friendship and shared experiences.

Let Sarah and David's story be a reminder that the world of Espresso Martinis is not just about the art of mixology, but about the connections forged and the memories created. It is a testament to the power of love, creativity, and the simple pleasures that bring us closer together.

As we raise our glasses, let us toast to the extraordinary journey of Sarah and David—a journey that has transformed lives, sparked creativity, and celebrated the timeless allure of Espresso Martinis. May their legacy live on, inspiring us all to embrace our passions, savor life's indulgences, and create lasting memories with those we hold dear. Cheers to love, friendship, and the magical world of Espresso Martinis.

Elevating Mixology to an Art Form

In the captivating tale of Sarah and David, we have witnessed the transformative power of passion, creativity, and a shared love for Espresso Martinis. Their journey has transcended the realm of mixology, elevating it to the status of an art form—an art form that awakens the senses sparks imagination, and fosters a profound connection between people and flavors.

Through their unwavering dedication and meticulous craftsmanship, Sarah and David have shown us that mixology is not merely a process of combining ingredients, but a deeply personal and expressive endeavor. They have embraced the nuances of coffee, the complexities of spirits, and the art of balance, breathing life into each cocktail they create.

Their meticulous attention to detail, from the selection of beans to the delicate garnishes, has transformed their cocktails into works of art—pieces that engage not only the taste buds but also the eyes and the soul. Every sip becomes a sensory experience, a moment of bliss that transports us to a realm where flavor becomes an exquisite form of self-expression.

In their quest to push the boundaries of mixology, Sarah and David have fearlessly experimented with unconventional ingredients, uncharted flavor combinations, and innovative techniques. They have challenged conventions, inviting us to embrace the unexpected, to break free from the confines of tradition, and to discover new dimensions of taste.

But perhaps the most remarkable aspect of Sarah and David's journey is the way in which they have invited others to join them in their pursuit of excellence. Their warmth, generosity, and willingness to share their knowledge have fostered a community of like-minded individuals, united by their passion for mixology and the desire to create memorable experiences.

Through their workshops, masterclasses, and gatherings, they have nurtured a space where budding mixologists can find inspiration, exchange ideas, and grow together. Sarah and David have become mentors, guiding others on their own artistic journeys, encouraging them to embrace their unique visions and explore the infinite possibilities within the realm of mixology.

As we bid farewell to Sarah and David, we are left with a profound appreciation for the art form they have elevated. Mixology, in their hands, has become a gateway to self-expression, a medium through which we can weave stories, evoke emotions, and create moments that transcend the ordinary.

So, let us raise our glasses one final time to honor Sarah and David—the guardians of the art of mixology. May their passion continue to inspire us, their creativity continue to ignite our imaginations, and their love for Espresso Martinis continue to bring people together in celebration of the beautiful, ever-evolving world of mixology —an art form that speaks to our souls, tantalizes our palates, and elevates our spirits. Cheers to the artists of flavor, the creators of magic, and the endless possibilities of mixology as an art form.

Crafting Memorable Moments of Indulgence

In the captivating narrative of Sarah and David, we have witnessed the transformative power of their love for Espresso Martinis, their dedication to the art of mixology, and their unwavering commitment to creating unforgettable moments of indulgence. As we conclude this remarkable journey, we are left with a profound appreciation for the way in which they have crafted memories that linger in the hearts and minds of all who have had the privilege of partaking in their world.

Sarah and David have shown us that the true essence of indulgence lies not only in the flavors that tantalize our taste buds but in the connections we form, the laughter we share, and the stories we weave. Through their meticulous attention to detail, their passion for craftsmanship, and their warm hospitality, they have created an immersive experience that transcends the ordinary and elevates the act of savoring a cocktail into a cherished moment of connection and celebration.

Each carefully crafted Espresso Martini is a vessel carrying the shared experiences, laughter, and conversations that have unfolded in the company of loved ones. It is a testament to the power of human connection and the extraordinary ability of a simple drink to foster joy, camaraderie, and a sense of belonging.

Sarah and David's dedication to their craft has touched the lives of those around them, leaving an indelible mark on their friends, family, and even strangers who have been fortunate enough to cross their path. Their commitment to excellence, their boundless creativity, and their genuine love for their guests have made every gathering a moment to be treasured—a memory that continues to resonate long after the last sip has been taken.

But their influence extends beyond their immediate circle. Through sharing their knowledge, hosting workshops, and embracing collaboration, they have inspired a ripple effect of indulgence, encouraging others to create their own moments of magic. Their legacy lives on in the homes of those they have touched, as friends and family come together to craft their own memorable moments of indulgence.

As we bid farewell to Sarah and David's world of crafting memorable moments of indulgence, we carry with us the lessons they have taught us—the importance of passion, dedication, and the art of creating experiences that linger in the hearts of others. They have shown us that true indulgence is not confined to the realm of cocktails; it is a celebration of life, love, and the beauty of human connection.

So let us raise our glasses in a final toast to Sarah and David, the architects of unforgettable experiences. May their journey continue to inspire us to infuse our own lives with a touch of indulgence, embrace the artistry that lies within each moment, and to savor the sweetness of life's pleasures.

Cheers to crafting memorable moments of indulgence, and to the infinite possibilities that await us as we embark on our own journeys of creating joy, connection, and lasting memories.

The Perfect Shake

As we bring our journey through the world of Sarah and David's Espresso Martinis to a close, we arrive at the heart of their craft—the perfect shake. It is in this seemingly simple yet essential act that their artistry truly shines, encapsulating the essence of their dedication, precision, and unwavering pursuit of excellence.

The perfect shake is a dance of elements—an intricate choreography that melds flavors, textures, and temperatures into a harmonious symphony. Sarah and David have honed their shaking technique to perfection, with just the right amount of vigor and finesse. The ice cubes collide with the cocktail shaker, creating a mesmerizing rhythm that amplifies the anticipation in the room.

The sound of the shake is music to their ears—a symphony of clinking ice, the subtle hiss of the liquids combining, and the steady beat of their passion. It is a sensory experience in itself, foreshadowing the delights that await when the cocktail is poured into a chilled glass.

The perfect shake is not just about the physical motion; it is an expression of their expertise and intuition. Through years of practice and experimentation, they have mastered the art of understanding the ingredients, the optimal duration of the shake, and the precise moment to stop. It is this intuitive understanding that sets their cocktails apart, ensuring a flawless balance of flavors and a velvety texture that glides over the palate.

Beyond the technical aspects, the perfect shake embodies the spirit of their craft—their dedication to craftsmanship, their pursuit of balance, and their unwavering attention to detail. It is a reflection of their commitment to creating moments of indulgence that go beyond the superficial, moments that leave a lasting impression on the senses and the soul.

But the perfect shake is not merely a means to an end; it is a journey in itself. It is an opportunity for Sarah and David to infuse their personal touch, their unique energy, and their love for their craft into every cocktail they create. It is a moment of connection, as the rhythm of their shake resonates with the anticipation of their guests, building excitement and setting the stage for the indulgent experience that awaits.

The perfect shake is a testament to the countless hours of practice, experimentation, and refinement that Sarah and David have dedicated to their art. It is a symbol of their unwavering pursuit of perfection—a pursuit that extends far beyond the boundaries of mixology and into the realm of creating memorable moments that transcend the ordinary.

As we bid adieu to the world of the perfect shake, let us carry with us the essence of Sarah and David's artistry— their dedication to craftsmanship, their commitment to balance, and their unwavering pursuit of excellence. Let us be inspired to embrace the pursuit of perfection in our own lives, to infuse our passions with the same level of devotion and care, and to savor every moment of indulgence that comes our way.

Cheers to the perfect shake, the embodiment of skill and passion, and to the joy and connection that can be found in every sip. May we all find our own version of the perfect shake, whether in mixology, in our personal endeavors, or in the art of living fully.

Garnishing Like a Pro and Tools of the Trade

As we come to the end of our exploration into the art of garnishing like a pro, we find ourselves mesmerized by the transformative power of a well-placed garnish. Sarah and David have shown us that the final flourish, the delicate touch of a garnish, has the ability to elevate a cocktail from ordinary to extraordinary.

Through their meticulous attention to detail and their keen eye for aesthetics, Sarah and David have taught us that garnishing is not merely a decorative afterthought. It is an art form that adds depth, complexity, and visual appeal to a cocktail, enticing all the senses and setting the stage for an unforgettable indulgence.

From the delicate twist of a citrus peel to the intricate arrangement of fresh herbs, each garnish is chosen with intention and purpose. It serves not only to enhance the flavors and aromas of the cocktail but also to tell a story—a story of craftsmanship, creativity, and the desire to create a truly memorable experience.

The art of garnishing, as showcased by Sarah and David, invites us to embrace our own creativity and explore the endless possibilities that lie within each ingredient. It encourages us to experiment, to step outside our comfort zones, and to embrace the joy of discovery as we uncover new flavors and combinations that tantalize the taste buds.

So as we bid adieu to the world of garnishing like a pro, let us carry with us the inspiration to infuse our own creations with the beauty and artistry of a well-executed garnish. Let us embrace the power of the final flourish, allowing it to ignite our imagination, surprise our senses, and create moments of indulgence that leave a lasting impression.

Tools of the Trade: As we conclude our journey into the realm of mixology tools, we are left with a profound appreciation for the impact that these seemingly mundane instruments can have on the art of cocktail-making. Sarah and David have shown us that the right tools not only enhance our ability to craft exceptional beverages but also elevate the entire experience.

From the sleek, well-balanced shaker that becomes an extension of their hands to the precision jigger that ensures accurate measurements, each tool plays a vital role in the pursuit of perfection. Sarah and David have honed their skills with these instruments, mastering the art of using them with grace, efficiency, and a touch of flair.

But beyond their functional value, the tools of the trade carry a symbolic significance. They represent the commitment, passion, and dedication that Sarah and David have poured into their craft. Each tool holds within it a wealth of knowledge and a sense of tradition, connecting them to a lineage of mixologists who have come before.

Moreover, these tools serve as a tangible reminder of the transformative power of passion and expertise. They inspire us to seek mastery in our own pursuits, to embrace the tools that aid us in our creative endeavors, and to approach our craft with the same level of care, precision, and enthusiasm.

As we bid farewell to the world of mixology tools, let us carry with us the appreciation for the role they play in the art of cocktail-making. Let us be inspired to seek out the tools that resonate with our own passions, to wield them with confidence and finesse, and to infuse our creations with the love and dedication that Sarah and David have so beautifully exemplified.

Cheers to the art of garnishing, to the tools that empower us, and to the countless possibilities that await us as we continue to explore the fascinating world of mixology. May we find joy in the details, embrace the tools of our trade, and craft moments of indulgence that leave a lasting impression on all who partake.

Acknowledgments

As we conclude this immersive journey through the art of Espresso Martinis, garnishing like a pro, and exploring the tools of the trade, it is important to express our heartfelt gratitude to those who have contributed to the creation of this captivating world.

First and foremost, we extend our deepest appreciation to Sarah and David, the visionaries behind these extraordinary experiences. Their passion, creativity, and dedication to their craft have provided the inspiration for this exploration, and their expertise has guided us through the intricacies of mixology.

Their willingness to share their knowledge and their unwavering commitment to excellence have enriched our understanding of the art of Espresso Martinis.

We would also like to extend our gratitude to the friends and family who have been a part of Sarah and David's journey. Their presence and support have added an invaluable element of joy and camaraderie to the world of indulgence that Sarah and David have crafted.

Their shared experiences, laughter, and cherished memories have underscored the true essence of hospitality and have reminded us of the power of togetherness.

Furthermore, we would like to acknowledge the mixologists, craftsmen, and artisans whose creations and contributions have shaped the landscape of the mixology world. Their innovations, expertise, and dedication to their respective crafts have paved the way for the artistry we have celebrated throughout this exploration.

They have left an indelible mark on the world of mixology, inspiring countless others to embark on their own journeys of creativity and indulgence.

Lastly, we express our gratitude to you, our readers and fellow enthusiasts of the craft. Your curiosity and eagerness to delve into the world of Espresso Martinis and mixology have made this journey worthwhile.

It is our hope that you have found inspiration, knowledge, and a renewed appreciation for the artistry that goes into creating moments of indulgence.

As we bid farewell to this immersive experience, we invite you to carry the spirit of Sarah and David's artistry, passion, and attention to detail into your own lives. May you continue to explore the world of mixology, infuse your creations with love and care, and savor every moment of indulgence with friends, family, and loved ones.

Cheers to the art of Espresso Martinis, the joy of garnishing, the tools of the trade, and the limitless possibilities that lie within the world of mixology. May your own journey be filled with creativity, discovery, and unforgettable moments of indulgence.

In the world of coffee, where the aroma of freshly brewed beans dances in the air and the anticipation of that first sip awakens the senses, there is a drink that stands out as a testament to the harmonious marriage of coffee and mixology—the Espresso Martini. This captivating libation, born from the passion and ingenuity of coffee lovers like Sarah and David, transcends the ordinary, elevating the coffee experience to a realm of indulgence and artistry.

As we conclude our exploration of Espresso Martinis, we are reminded of the profound connection that coffee lovers share—a bond that goes beyond the surface-level appreciation of the bean. It is a connection rooted in the appreciation for the craftsmanship and artistry that goes into each sip. It is a shared enthusiasm for the complexities of flavor, the velvety textures, and the transformative power of coffee.

Through the journey of Espresso Martinis, we have discovered that this enchanting cocktail is more than just a drink—it is a vessel of shared moments and heartfelt connections. It is the catalyst for laughter-filled evenings, intimate conversations, and celebrations of life's milestones. It has the power to bring people together, creating a tapestry of memories woven with the threads of coffee-infused joy.

For coffee lovers, the Espresso Martini is a celebration of their deep-rooted passion—a testament to their commitment to seeking perfection in every cup. It is a testament to their adventurous spirit, as they push the boundaries of creativity, exploring new flavors, and daring to experiment with unconventional ingredients. It is an embodiment of their unwavering dedication to the craft of coffee and mixology.

But above all, the Espresso Martini is a love letter to the very essence of coffee. It is a testament to the magic that happens when the richness of espresso, the vibrancy of spirits, and the artistry of mixology converge in a single glass. It is a sensory experience that envelops you in its embrace, awakening your taste buds, tantalizing your senses, and leaving an indelible mark on your soul.

To all the coffee lovers out there, let the Espresso Martini be a reminder of the beauty that lies within your passion. Embrace the art of mixology, explore the depths of flavors, and continue to be captivated by the possibilities that coffee presents. Share your love for coffee, gather your friends, and let the Espresso Martini be the centerpiece of your gatherings—a symbol of togetherness, laughter, and unforgettable moments.

As we bid farewell to this exploration of Espresso Martinis, we carry with us a profound appreciation for the artistry, commitment, and joy that coffee lovers infuse into every sip. Let us raise our glasses, clink them together, and toast to the enduring love affair between coffee and mixology. May your cups be forever filled with the liquid poetry that is the Espresso Martini, and may your coffee journey continue to inspire and delight.

Cheers, dear coffee lovers, to the magic of Espresso Martinis and the unending pleasure found in every sip. May your love for coffee be as boundless as the flavors that dance upon your palate.

As we come to the end of this enchanting journey, let us take a moment to reflect on the extraordinary world of coffee and the artistry it inspires. The Espresso Martini, with its captivating allure and harmonious blend of flavors, has been our guide through this exploration, inviting us to embrace indulgence, celebrate craftsmanship, and forge lasting connections.

In the realm of coffee lovers, we find a community bonded by a shared passion, an unspoken understanding of the depth and complexity that lies within a humble coffee bean. It is a world where conversations flow effortlessly, fueled by the invigorating elixir that brings us together. It is a space where friendships are forged, memories are created, and moments of pure indulgence are savored.

As we bid adieu, let us carry with us the spirit of the Espresso Martini—an emblem of creativity, elegance, and the pursuit of perfection. Let it serve as a reminder that within the realms of mixology, coffee transcends its traditional form, becoming an exquisite canvas for innovation and artistry.

May the flavors we have discovered linger on our palates, reminding us of the intricacies that unfold with each sip. May the stories of Sarah and David, their passion for coffee, and their devotion to the art of mixology, continue to inspire us to elevate our own coffee experiences.

In the grand tapestry of life, coffee holds a special place—a catalyst for connection, a conduit for expression, and a source of pure pleasure. It is the elixir that fuels our dreams, awakens our senses, and envelops us in a comforting embrace.

So, dear coffee lovers, as we bid farewell to this exploration of the Espresso Martini, let us cherish the memories we have created, the flavors we have savored, and the connections we have forged. Let us continue to celebrate coffee in all its forms, and honor the artisans who bring its magic to life.

May your coffee adventures be filled with countless moments of indulgence, shared laughter, and profound appreciation for the wonders that lie within each cup. And may the art of the Espresso Martini forever inspire you to seek beauty, elevate your craft, and embrace the extraordinary.

Until we meet again, may your coffee journeys be abundant with discoveries, your taste buds be tantalized by new flavors, and your hearts be warmed by the love that brews within each pot. Cheers to the art of coffee, the magic of mixology, and the enduring joy they bring to our lives.

Farewell for now, dear coffee lovers. May the allure of the Espresso Martini guide you to new heights of indulgence, creativity, and connection. Until our paths cross again, may your cups be filled with the richness of life and the everlasting aroma of coffee.

With heartfelt gratitude and a shared love for the bean, we bid you adieu.

There are countless reasons to fall in love with the Espresso Martini. Here are just a few of the many things to adore about this delightful coffee cocktail:

1. Perfect balance: The Espresso Martini achieves a harmonious balance between the bold, rich flavors of espresso and the smooth, velvety sweetness of spirits. It is a marriage of contrasts that tantalizes the taste buds.

2. Indulgent decadence: Sipping on an Espresso Martini is like treating yourself to a luxurious dessert in liquid form. It is a decadent indulgence that satisfies both the craving for a coffee fix and the desire for a sophisticated cocktail.

3. Energizing effect: With the caffeine kick from the espresso, the Espresso Martini not only delights the palate but also provides a boost of energy. It's the perfect pick-me-up to keep the night going or to start an evening of celebration.

4. Versatility: The Espresso Martini is a versatile cocktail that can be enjoyed in various settings. It is equally suited for intimate gatherings, trendy cocktail bars, or even as a post-dinner digestif. Its adaptability ensures it always has a place in the repertoire of coffee and cocktail lovers.

5. Artistic presentation: The Espresso Martini is often adorned with eye-catching garnishes and served in elegant martini glasses. Its visual appeal adds to the overall experience, making it a cocktail that is as pleasing to the eyes as it is to the taste buds.

6. Endless variations: While the classic recipe is a masterpiece in itself, the Espresso Martini offers

endless opportunities for experimentation. From flavored liqueurs to innovative twists with unexpected ingredients, there is a world of possibilities to explore and create your own signature version.

7. A social catalyst: The Espresso Martini has a remarkable ability to bring people together. It serves as a conversation starter, a shared experience, and a catalyst for memorable moments with friends, family, or even fellow coffee and cocktail enthusiasts.

8. A celebration of craftsmanship: Crafting the perfect Espresso Martini requires precision, skill, and a deep appreciation for the artistry of coffee and mixology. It is a testament to the dedication and expertise of the bartenders and coffee aficionados who pour their heart and soul into each creation.

9. A sensory journey: From the enticing aroma of freshly brewed espresso to the velvety texture that coats the palate, the Espresso Martini takes you on a sensory journey like no other. Every sip is a moment of bliss that engages all your senses.

10. The embodiment of coffee's allure: The Espresso Martini encapsulates the essence of coffee's allure—the intoxicating aroma, the depth of flavors, and the ability to ignite passion and creativity. It is a celebration of coffee's enduring appeal and its ability to captivate us in both its pure and transformed forms.

These are just a few reasons why the Espresso Martini holds a special place in the hearts of coffee and cocktail lovers around the world. Its combination of coffee's soul-stirring qualities and mixology's creative touch makes it a beloved and unforgettable drink. So raise your glass and toast to the beauty and brilliance of the Espresso Martini!

As the seasons change and new trends emerge, there is one drink that stands out as the favorite of the moment—the Espresso Martini. Here's why this delightful cocktail has captured the hearts of many and become the go-to choice for the season:

1. The perfect balance of flavors: The Espresso Martini strikes a perfect balance between the robust, bitter notes of espresso and the smooth, sweet undertones of spirits and liqueurs. It is a harmonious blend that pleases the palate and satisfies the taste buds.

2. An invigorating pick-me-up: With its infusion of espresso, the Espresso Martini offers more than just a delicious drink. It provides a revitalizing boost of energy, making it an ideal choice for those seeking a little extra perk during the season's busy days and vibrant nights.

3. A versatile companion: Whether you're attending a glamorous soirée, hosting a dinner party, or simply unwinding after a long day, the Espresso Martini is a versatile companion that suits any occasion. Its sophistication and allure make it a stylish choice that complements both casual gatherings and formal affairs.

4. A sensory delight: From the moment the aroma of freshly brewed espresso wafts through the air to the first sip that dances on your tongue, the Espresso

Martini is a sensory delight. The velvety texture, the rich flavors, and the enticing fragrance combine to create a truly immersive experience for all your senses.

5. A symbol of indulgence: The season often calls for moments of indulgence and celebration, and the Espresso Martini is the perfect embodiment of that. Its luxurious nature and decadent profile make it an ideal treat to savor and enjoy during special occasions or to elevate everyday moments.

6. Endless possibilities for customization: While the classic Espresso Martini recipe is beloved, the season invites experimentation and exploration. With a wide range of spirits, liqueurs, and flavorings available, you can personalize your Espresso Martini to suit your taste preferences and create your own signature twist.

7. The perfect marriage of coffee and cocktail culture: The Espresso Martini seamlessly merges the worlds of coffee and mixology, appealing to both coffee enthusiasts and cocktail connoisseurs alike. It celebrates the artistry and craftsmanship of both disciplines, creating a unique and captivating beverage that bridges these two beloved realms.

8. A social sensation: The Espresso Martini has a way of bringing people together and igniting conversations. Its allure sparks intrigue and serves as a great conversation starter, making it a delightful companion for social gatherings and a catalyst for unforgettable moments with friends and loved ones.

9. A touch of elegance: The Espresso Martini exudes an air of sophistication and elegance that adds a touch of glamour to any occasion. Its presentation in a sleek martini glass, often garnished with a coffee

bean or a twist of citrus, elevates its visual appeal and makes it a true showstopper.

10.A taste of pure pleasure: Ultimately, the reason why the Espresso Martini has become the favorite drink of the season is that it delivers pure pleasure. Its combination of coffee's allure, mixology's artistry, and the sheer delight it brings with each sip make it a drink that is cherished, savored, and remembered.

So, as the season unfolds, embrace the charm of the Espresso Martini. Indulge in its flavors, share it with loved ones, and celebrate the moments that make life extraordinary. Raise your glass and toast to the irresistible allure of the Espresso Martini—the favorite drink of the season.

We warmly invite you, coffee enthusiasts and mixology aficionados, to embark on an immersive journey through the captivating world of **ECoffeeFinder.com**.

This digital haven is designed to cater to your deepest passions, providing a personal sanctuary where you can indulge in the art of coffee and mixology at your own pace.

Step into a realm where the rich aromas of freshly brewed coffee fill the air and the clinking of cocktail shakers sets the rhythm of your exploration. Here, you'll find a wealth of resources, tailored recommendations, and a vibrant community eager to share their experiences and expertise.

At ECoffeeFinder.com, your quest for the perfect cup of coffee is met with a vast array of knowledge, from selecting the finest beans to mastering brewing techniques that unlock their true potential. Dive into captivating articles, immersive videos, and interactive tutorials that unveil the secrets of crafting exceptional coffee beverages.

But the journey doesn't end there. Immerse yourself in the alchemy of mixology, as ECoffeeFinder.com unveils a trove of carefully curated cocktail recipes, expert tips, and captivating stories that celebrate the art of crafting exquisite libations. Explore the world of flavors, experiment with unique combinations, and unlock your inner mixologist as you create drinks that will delight and inspire.

Beyond the wealth of information, ECoffeeFinder.com is a haven for like-minded enthusiasts like yourself. Connect with fellow coffee lovers and mixology mavens, share your discoveries, and engage in lively discussions that deepen your appreciation for these art forms. Build lasting connections, exchange ideas, and ignite your creativity as you become part of a dynamic community that thrives on the love of coffee and mixology.

So, dear friend, we invite you to seize this opportunity to immerse yourself in a world where passion and craftsmanship converge. Visit ECoffeeFinder.com and allow yourself to be whisked away on a personalized journey of indulgence and discovery.

Raise your cup, shake up your favorite libation, and embark on an adventure that transcends the ordinary. At ECoffeeFinder.com, the world of coffee and mixology awaits, ready to ignite your senses, expand your horizons, and enrich your appreciation for the remarkable artistry that lies within each sip and shake.

Cheers to your unique journey, dear friend. May it be filled with unforgettable moments, delightful flavors, and the joy of sharing your newfound expertise with those who appreciate the finer things in life.

Learn more about E Coffee Finder Online:

https://linktr.ee/ECoffeeFinder

Made in United States
Orlando, FL
28 December 2024

56668681R00046